LEARN BOOTSTRAP WEB DESIGN

FROM SCHOOL LEVEL TO EVERYONE

AADISHREE AVINASH PAGAR

I would like to dedicate this book to most loving, caring and supportive my mummy and pappa,

dedicated to all **students,**

dedicated to all students **studied in struggle,**

and those students who are **hungry for knowledge,**

also for those student who are always eager to **innovate new things.**

Miss. Aadishree Avinash Pagar

Contents

1. Introduction To Web Designing	1
2. About Bootstrap	3
3. Page Layouts	5
4. Grid Systems	8
5. Typography	11
6. Bootstrap Forms	15
7. Colors	19
8. Images	23
9. Tables	26
10. Buttons	42
11. Button Groups	47
12. Labels	50
13. Dropdowns	52
14. Glyphicons	54
15. List Groups	57
16. Jumbotron	59
17. Badges	61
18. Alerts	66
19. Panels	69
20. Cards	71
21. Breadcrumbs	76
22. Tooltips	78
23. Navbar	81
24. Carousal	84
25. Modal	87
26. Progress Bar	89

CHAPTER ONE

Introduction to Web Designing

Topics covered

1. **What is Web Designing?**
2. **How to Designing Web Page?**

Web designing is having a lot of definitions as per every author and book. I describe web designing as per my experience. Web designing is the process of building or designing a web page as per the requirement with the help of images, text, colors, fonts, mark-up language, graphical elements and videos. Every website is having its own web page structure. Website contains pages like home page, information page, picture gallery, feedback page and contact us page. The person or professional who develop this process is called web designer. To develop website, HTML, CSS and Bootstrap languages are used.

Web site designing process includes imagination and ideas to give information to end user. Every website should follow some rules to develop proper web site. Let us learn some of the rules.

1. Website should be **user friendly**.
2. It should be attractive **to keep more visitors**.
3. It should be **responsive**i.e. Works on gadgets like phone, tablet, laptop and desktop properly.

4. The website should have **easy-to-read fonts.**
5. The website has attractive **color schemes.**
6. The website should **load fast to be responsive.**

In next chapter we will see the web designing process and learn bootstrap class and components of website.

CHAPTER TWO

About Bootstrap

Topics Covered

What is bootstrap?

Use of Bootstrap

Versions of Bootstrap

Install Bootstrap.

Bootstrap – Bootstrap is the most popular free and open-source HTML, CSS and JavaScript framework, is used to develop **responsive** websites and is also known as **mobile-first** websites.

Bootstrap was actually named as **Twitter Blueprint**. It is developed by **Mark Otto** and **Jacob Thornton** at Twitter incorporation.

Bootstrap 1

It is open-source project and it renamed Twitter blueprint to Bootstrap. Bootstrap 1 is released on 20 August 2011.

Bootstrap 2

Bootstrap 2 was released on 31 January 2012.

Bootstrap 3

Bootstrap 3 was released on 19 August 2013.

Bootstrap 4

Bootstrap 4 was released on 29 October 2014.

Bootstrap 5

Bootstrap 5 is the latest version of bootstrap. **Bootstrap 5** was released 5 May 2021. Bootstrap 5 is also free to use and can be downloaded from the website.

Implement Bootstrap 5 In a Website.

It's very simple to use Bootstrap 5 in your website. There are two methods –

1. Download Bootstrap 5 from www.getbootstrap.com official website.
2. Add CSS and JS file from **Content Delivery Network** in your webpage. Links are available on www.getbootstrap.com official website

Using second option adds below two files in head section of webpage.

```
<link href="https://cdn.jsdelivr.net/npm/bootstrap@5.1.3/dist/css/bootstrap.min.css" rel="stylesheet">
<script src="https://cdn.jsdelivr.net/npm/bootstrap@5.1.3/dist/js/bootstrap.bundle.min.js"></script>
```

First Bootstrap Program –

To write bootstrap program we can use Notepad text editor. Notepad is easily found in every computer. Also we can use Notepad++, Sublime type text editors to write code.

Following steps follow to create bootstrap code.

1. Open Notepad or Notepad++ or any text editor.
2. Click on **File** menu. Select **New** submenu option.
3. **Write** down your Bootstrap program or code.
4. Save file with **.html** extension.
5. Double click on saved file your program will open on default browser.

Remember – Follow these steps to create Bootstrap Program.

CHAPTER THREE

Page Layouts

Topics Covered

    About Page Layout

    Fixed width Page Layout

    Full Width Page Layout

    Responsive Pages

Page Layout - To manage page layout in bootstrap container classes available. By using container class, we display page content as per requirement. Page layout changes as per the screen size change. Some screen sizes are -

1. **Extra small** screen size
2. **Small** screen size
3. **Medium** screen size
4. **Large** screen size
5. **Extra-large** screen size

Fixed width page layout–To display **Fixed Width Page Layout** we have to use **.container** class which provides a responsive fixed width container.

3.1- Write a Bootstrap program for introduction to Page Layout.

```
<html>
<head>
<title>Bootstrap - Page Layout</title>
```

```
<link    href="https://cdn.jsdelivr.net/npm/bootstrap@5.1.3/
dist/css/bootstrap.min.css" rel="stylesheet">
<script    src="https://cdn.jsdelivr.net/npm/bootstrap@5.1.3/
dist/js/bootstrap.bundle.min.js"></script>
</head>
<body>
<div class="container">
<h1>Page Layout</h1>
<p>This is container class example. </p>
</div>
</body>
</html>
```

Page Layout

This is container class example

Program Output3.1- Container Class Example

Full Width Page Layout – To display **Full Width Page Layout** we have to use **.container-fluid** class which provides a responsive full width container. It provides 100 percentage page width i.e., entire width of the screen.

3.2 - Write a Bootstrap program for introduction Full Width to Page Layout.

```
<html>
<head>
<title>Bootstrap - Page Layout</title>
<link    href="https://cdn.jsdelivr.net/npm/bootstrap@5.1.3/
dist/css/bootstrap.min.css" rel="stylesheet">
<script    src="https://cdn.jsdelivr.net/npm/bootstrap@5.1.3/
dist/js/bootstrap.bundle.min.js"></script>
</head>
<body>
<div class="container-fluid">
```

```
<h1>Page Layout</h1>
<p>This is container-fluid class example.</p>
</div>
</body>
</html>
```

Page Layout

This is container-fluid class example.

Program Output3.2 - Container Fluid Class Example.

Responsive Pages –
Responsive web pages means to design web page in a way that it looks good on all types of devices by arranged or adjust size itself automatically. The devices or gadgets like from mobiles, tabs to laptop and desktop computers.

CHAPTER FOUR

Grid Systems

Grid system in Bootstrap 5.

Bootstrap 5 provides powerful concept of Grid System to design and arrange the page content.

Every row is divided into **12 columns**.

These 12 columns are arranged in different style .

Create 1 column – By creating group all 12 columns together.

Create 2 equal columns – By creating group of 6-columns together.

Create 3 equal columns – By creating group of 4-columns together.

Create 4 equal columns – By creating group of 3-columns together.

Create 6 equal columns – By creating group of 2-columns.

Create 12 equal columns – By creating columns individually.

Create a row using this code - <div class="row">

The bootstrap 5 grid system having classes -

SM - small devices

MD – medium devices

LG – large devices

XL – extra-large devices

XXL – extra extra-large devices

4.1 - Write a Bootstrap Program To Create Four Equal Columns.

<html>

<head>

```html
<title>Bootstrap - Create Columns</title>
<link href="https://cdn.jsdelivr.net/npm/bootstrap@5.1.3/dist/css/bootstrap.min.css" rel="stylesheet">
<script src="https://cdn.jsdelivr.net/npm/bootstrap@5.1.3/dist/js/bootstrap.bundle.min.js"></script>
</head>
<body>
<div class="container">
<h1>Introduction To Columns</h1>
<p>Create four equal columns</p>
<div class="row">
<div class="col">Column-1</div>
<div class="col">Column-2</div>
<div class="col">Column-3</div>
<div class="col">Column-4</div>
</div>
</div>
</body>
</html>
```

Introduction To Columns

Create four equal columns

Column-1 Column-2 Column-3 Column-4

Program Output 4.1 - Four columns are created in a row.

4.2 Program to create Two responsive unequal columns.

```html
<html>
<head>
<title>Bootstrap - Columns</title>
<link href="https://cdn.jsdelivr.net/npm/bootstrap@5.1.3/dist/css/bootstrap.min.css" rel="stylesheet">
<script src="https://cdn.jsdelivr.net/npm/bootstrap@5.1.3/dist/js/bootstrap.bundle.min.js"></script>
</head>
```

```
<body>
<div class="container">
<h1>Columns</h1>
<p>Create Two Unequal Responsive Columns</p>
<div class="row">
<div class="col-sm-8">Column-1</div>
<div class="col-sm-4">Column-2</div>
</div>
</div>
</body>
</html>
```

Program Output 4.2 - Create two enequal columns.

CHAPTER FIVE

Typography

Topics Covered –
What is typography
Text Alignment
Abbreviations
Small class
In typography section covers the formatting of text content such as headings of content, paragraphs and blockquotes.

Bootstrap 5 provides HTML headings from <h1> to <h6> header styles.

<p class="h1"> This is Bootstrap heading with h1 style class</p>
<p class="h2">This is Bootstrap heading with h2 style class</p>
<p class="h3">This is Bootstrap heading with h3 style class</p>
<p class="h4">This is Bootstrap heading with h4 style class</p>
<p class="h5">This is Bootstrap heading with h5 style class</p>
<p class="h6">This is Bootstrap heading with h6 style class</p>
Displays with bolder font-weight and responsive font-size.

Text Alignment –

Bootstrap provides three different classes for text alignment to align text- left, center and right.

5.1 Write a program to display Text Alignment.
<html>
<head>
<title>Bootstrap - Typography</title>
<link href="https://cdn.jsdelivr.net/npm/bootstrap@5.1.3/dist/css/bootstrap.min.css" rel="stylesheet">

```
<script       src="https://cdn.jsdelivr.net/npm/bootstrap@5.1.3/
dist/js/bootstrap.bundle.min.js"></script>
</head>
<body>
<div class="container">
<h1>Text Alignment</h1>
<p>Introduction To Text Alignment</p>
<div class="row">
<div class="col-sm-4">
<p class="text-start">Introduction to Left aligned text</p>
</div>
<div class="col-sm-4">
<p class="text-center">Introduction to Center aligned text</p>
</div>
<div class="col-sm-4">
<p class="text-end">Introduction to Right aligned text</p>
</div>
</div>
</div>
</body>
</html>
```


Program Output5.1 - Text Alignment

Abbreviations –
The abbr element provides markup abbreviations or acronym.

```
<html>
<head>
<title>Bootstrap - Typography</title>
<link       href="https://cdn.jsdelivr.net/npm/bootstrap@5.1.3/
dist/css/bootstrap.min.css" rel="stylesheet">
```

```
<script    src="https://cdn.jsdelivr.net/npm/bootstrap@5.1.3/
dist/js/bootstrap.bundle.min.js"></script>
</head>
<body>
<div class="container">
<h1>Abbreviations </h1>
<p>The abbr element provides to markup abbreviations or
acronym </p>
<div class="row">
<div class="col-sm-8">
<p>The <abbr title="World Wide Web">WWW</abbr> is used
for the information retrieval service for the internet.</p>
</div>
</div>
</div>
</body>
</html>
```

Abbreviations

The abbr element provides to markup abbreviations or acronym

The WWW is used for the information retrieval service for the internet.

Program Output 5.2 - Abbreviations

Small element or small class– it provides or it is used for the purpose of to create a smaller text, secondary text in any heading.

```
<p    class="h1">Bootstrap    heading    with    <small>h1    style
class</small></p>
<p    class="h2">Bootstrap    heading    with    <small>h2    style
class</small></p>
<p    class="h3">Bootstrap    heading    with    <small>h3    style
class</small></p>
<p    class="h4">Bootstrap    heading    with    <small>h4    style
class</small></p>
```

```
<p class="h5">Bootstrap heading with <small>h5 style class</small></p>
<p class="h6">Bootstrap heading with <small>h6 style class</small></p>
```

CHAPTER SIX

Bootstrap Forms

Bootstrap forms build using various components like Label, Textbox, Text area, Button etc. we can create or design different types of forms using these components.

Label and Textbox

6.1-Write a Bootstrap Program to Create Label and Textbox.

```
<html>
<head>
<title>Bootstrap - Forms</title>
<link      href="https://cdn.jsdelivr.net/npm/bootstrap@5.1.3/
dist/css/bootstrap.min.css" rel="stylesheet">
<script      src="https://cdn.jsdelivr.net/npm/bootstrap@5.1.3/
dist/js/bootstrap.bundle.min.js"></script>
</head>
<body>
<div class="container">
<h1>Form</h1>
<p>Create Textbox and Labels</p>
<div class="row">
<div class="col-sm-4">
<label for="name" class="form-label">First Name:</label>
<input      type="text"      class="form-control"      id="fname"
placeholder="Enter First Name" name="fname">
</div>
<div class="col-sm-4">
<label for="name" class="form-label">Middle Name:</label>
```

```
<input      type="text"      class="form-control"      id="mname"
placeholder="Enter Middle Name" name="mname">
   </div>
   <div class="col-sm-4">
   <label for="name" class="form-label">Last Name:</label>
   <input      type="text"      class="form-control"      id="lname"
placeholder="Enter Last Name" name="lname">
   </div>
   </div>
   </div>
   </body>
   </html>
```

Form

Create Textbox and Labels

First Name: Middle Name   Last Name

Enter First Name   Enter Middle Name   Enter Last Name

Program Output 6.1 - Create Label and Textbox

6.2 - Write a Bootstrap Program to Create a Login Form.

```
<html>
<head>
<title>Bootstrap - Forms</title>
<link      href="https://cdn.jsdelivr.net/npm/bootstrap@5.1.3/
dist/css/bootstrap.min.css" rel="stylesheet">
<script      src="https://cdn.jsdelivr.net/npm/bootstrap@5.1.3/
dist/js/bootstrap.bundle.min.js"></script>
</head>
<body>
<div class="container">
<h1>Form</h1>
<p>Login Form</p>
<div class="row">
<div class="col-sm-4">
```

```html
<label for="username" class="form-label">User Name:</label>
<input type="text" class="form-control" id="username" placeholder="Enter User Name" name="username">
</div>
</div>
<div class="row">
<div class="col-sm-4">
<label for="password" class="form-label">Password:</label>
<input type="password" class="form-control" id="password" placeholder="Enter Password" name="password">
</div>
</div>
<div class="row">
<div class="col-sm-4">
<label class="form-check-label">
<input class="form-check-input" type="checkbox" name="remember"> Remember me
</label>
</div>
</div>
<button type="submit" class="btn btn-primary">Submit</button>
</div>
</body>
</html>
```

Program Output 6.2 - Login Form

6.3 - Write a Bootstrap Program to Create Textarea.

```html
<html>
<head>
<title>Bootstrap - Forms</title>
<link      href="https://cdn.jsdelivr.net/npm/bootstrap@5.1.3/
dist/css/bootstrap.min.css" rel="stylesheet">
<script     src="https://cdn.jsdelivr.net/npm/bootstrap@5.1.3/
dist/js/bootstrap.bundle.min.js"></script>
</head>
<body>
<div class="container">
<h1>Form</h1>
<p>Texr Area Component</p>
<div class="row">
<div class="col-sm-4">
<label for="comment">Feedback:</label>
<textarea      class="form-control"     rows="5"     id="feedback"
name="text"></textarea>
</div>
</div>
</br>
<button           type="submit"          class="btn          btn-
primary">Submit</button>
</div>
</body>
</html>
```


Program Output 6.3 - Text Area

Colors

Colors plays most important role in the bootstrap 5 web page designing as a background, text, heading and different kinds of icon colors.

Background colors having following classes.

bg-light

bg-dark

bg-primary

bg-secondary

bg-info

bg-warning

bg-success

bg-danger

7.1-Write aBootstrap program to show various background colors.

```
<html>
<head>
<title>Bootstrap - Colors</title>
<link     href="https://cdn.jsdelivr.net/npm/bootstrap@5.1.3/dist/css/bootstrap.min.css" rel="stylesheet">
<script     src="https://cdn.jsdelivr.net/npm/bootstrap@5.1.3/dist/js/bootstrap.bundle.min.js"></script>
</head>
<body>
<div class="container">
<h1>Colors</h1>
```

```html
<p>Background Colors</p>
<div class="row">
<div class="col-sm-6">
<p class="bg-light text-dark">Background of this text uses - bg-light class.</p>
<p class="bg-dark text-white">Background of this text uses - bg-dark class.</p>
<p class="bg-primary text-white">Background of this text uses - bg-primary class.</p>
<p class="bg-secondary text-white">Background of this text uses - bg-secondary class.</p>
<p class="bg-info text-white">Background of this text uses - bg-info class.</p>
<p class="bg-warning text-white">Background of this text uses - bg-warning class.</p>
<p class="bg-success text-white">Background of this text uses - bg-success class.</p>
<p class="bg-danger text-white">Background of this text uses - bg-danger class.</p>
</div>
</div>
</div>
</body>
</html>
```

Colors

Background Colors

Background of this text uses - bg-light class

Background of this text uses - bg-dark class

Background of this text uses - bg-primary class.

Background of this text uses - bg-secondary class.

Background of this text uses - bg-info class

Background of this text uses - bg-success class.

Background of this text uses - bg-danger class.

Program Output 7.1- Create various background colors.

Text colors having following classes -
text-primary
text-secondary
text-info
text-success
text-warning
text-danger
text-muted
text-white
text-dark
text-body

7.2-Write a Bootstrap program to show various text colors.

```
<html>
<head>
<title>Bootstrap - Colors</title>
<link     href="https://cdn.jsdelivr.net/npm/bootstrap@5.1.3/
dist/css/bootstrap.min.css" rel="stylesheet">
<script     src="https://cdn.jsdelivr.net/npm/bootstrap@5.1.3/
dist/js/bootstrap.bundle.min.js"></script>
</head>
<body>
<div class="container">
<h1>Colors</h1>
<p>Text Colors</p>
<div class="row">
<div class="col-sm-6">
<p  class="text-primary">Current  text  having  text-primary
class.</p>
<p class="text-secondary">Current text having text-secondary
class.</p>
<p class="text-info">Current text having text-info class.</p>
<p  class="text-success">Current  text  having  text-success
class.</p>
```

```
    <p class="text-warning">Current text having text-warning
class.</p>
    <p class="text-danger">Current text having text-danger
class.</p>
    <p class="text-muted">Current text having text-muted
class.</p>
    <p class="text-white">Current text having text-white class.</p>
    <p class="text-dark">Current text having text-dark class.</p>
    <p class="text-body">Current text having text-body class.</p>
    </div>
    </div>
    </div>
    </body>
    </html>
```

Colors

Text Colors

Current text having text-primary class

Current text having text-secondary class

Current text having text-success class

Current text having text-warning class

Current text having text-danger class

Current text having text-muted class

Current text having text-dark class

Current text having text-body class

Program Output 7.2- Display text with diferent colors.

CHAPTER EIGHT

Images

Bootstrap 5 provides classes for display images in attractive manner in web page design.

Images displayed using following classes.

Thumbnail - Img-thumbnail class displays image in thumbnail style.

Circle - rounded-circle class displays image in circle style.

Rounded corners – rounded class displays rounded corners to the image.

8.1 - Write a Bootstrap Program to Show Image Classes.

```
<html>
<head>
<title>Bootstrap - Images</title>
<link href="https://cdn.jsdelivr.net/npm/bootstrap@5.1.3/dist/css/bootstrap.min.css" rel="stylesheet">
<script src="https://cdn.jsdelivr.net/npm/bootstrap@5.1.3/dist/js/bootstrap.bundle.min.js"></script>
</head>
<body>
<div class="container">
<h1>Images</h1>
<p>Image classes</p>
<div class="row">
<div class="col-sm-4">
<img src="1.jpg" class="img-thumbnail" alt="Water is life">
</div>
```

```
</div>
<div class="row">
<div class="col-sm-4">
<img src="2.jpg" class="rounded-circle" alt="Water is life">
</div>
</div>
<div class="row">
<div class="col-sm-4">
<img src="3.jpg" class="rounded" alt="Water is life">
</div>
</div>
</div>
</body>
</html>
```

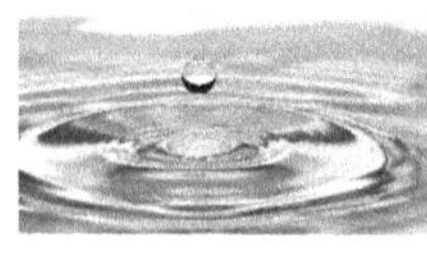
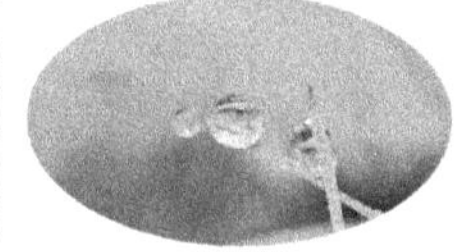

Program Output 8.1- Display image with different styles.

Image Alignment

float-start – Align image In left hand side.

float-end – Align image in right hand side

mx-auto – Align image in center.

8.2 - Write a Bootstrap Program to Show Image Alignment.

```
<html>
<head>
<title>Bootstrap - Images</title>
<link    href="https://cdn.jsdelivr.net/npm/bootstrap@5.1.3/dist/css/bootstrap.min.css" rel="stylesheet">
<script   src="https://cdn.jsdelivr.net/npm/bootstrap@5.1.3/dist/
```

```html
js/bootstrap.bundle.min.js"></script>
</head>
<body>
<div class="container">
<h1>Images</h1>
<p>Image Alignment</p>
<div class="row">
<div class="col-sm-4 mx-auto">
<img src="3.jpg" class="rounded" alt="water is life" style="width:100%">
</div>
</div>
    <div class="row">
<div class="col-sm-12">
<img src="1.jpg" class="img-thumbnail float-start" alt="Water is life" width="350" height="200">
    <img src="2.jpg" class="rounded-circle float-end" alt="Water is life" width="350" height="200"> </div>
</div>
</div>
</body>
</html>
```

CHAPTER NINE

Tables

Topics covered
What is Table?

1. **Basic Table -**
2. **Bordered Table -**
3. **Borderless Table -**
4. **Responsive Table -**
5. **Striped Rows Table -**
6. **Hover Rows Table -**
7. **Black/Dark Table -**
8. **Contextual Classes -**

The table is a combination of rows and columns.
9.1 - Write a program to display Basic Table.

```
<html>
<head>
<title>Bootstrap - Tables</title>
<link href="https://cdn.jsdelivr.net/npm/bootstrap@5.1.3/dist/css/bootstrap.min.css" rel="stylesheet">
<script src="https://cdn.jsdelivr.net/npm/bootstrap@5.1.3/dist/js/bootstrap.bundle.min.js"></script>
</head>
<body>
<div class="container">
<h1>Tables</h1>
```

```
<p>Basic Table</p>
<div class="row">
<div class="col-sm-6">
<table class="table">
<thead>
<tr>
<th>Firstname</th>
<th>Lastname</th>
<th>Email</th>
</tr>
</thead>
<tbody>
<tr>
<td>Taniya</td>
<td>Sevakramani</td>
<td>taniya@gmail.com</td>
</tr>
<tr>
<td>Aaditi</td>
<td>Gunjal</td>
<td>aaditi@gmail.com</td>
</tr>
<tr>
<td>Spandan</td>
<td>Gite</td>
<td>spandan@gmail.com</td>
</tr>
<tr>
<td>Kavya</td>
<td>Kanjode</td>
<td>kavya@gmail.com</td>
</tr>
</tbody>
</table>
</div>
```

```
</div>
</div>
</body>
</html>
```

Tables

Basic Table

Firstname	Lastname	Email
Taniya	Sevakramani	taniya@gmail.com
Aaditi	Gunjal	aaditi@gmail.com
Spandan	Gite	spandan@gmail.com
Kavya	Kanjode	kavya@gmail.com

Program Output 9.1- Basic Table

9.2- Write a program to display Bordered Table.

```
<html>
<head>
<title>Bootstrap - Tables</title>
<link     href="https://cdn.jsdelivr.net/npm/bootstrap@5.1.3/
dist/css/bootstrap.min.css" rel="stylesheet">
<script     src="https://cdn.jsdelivr.net/npm/bootstrap@5.1.3/
dist/js/bootstrap.bundle.min.js"></script>
</head>
<body>
<div class="container">
<h1>Tables</h1>
<p>Bordered Table</p>
<div class="row">
<div class="col-sm-6">
<table class="table table-bordered">
<thead>
<tr>
<th>Firstname</th>
<th>Lastname</th>
<th>Email</th>
```

```html
</tr>
</thead>
<tbody>
<tr>
<td>Taniya</td>
<td>Sevakramani</td>
<td>taniya@gmail.com</td>
</tr>
<tr>
<td>Aaditi</td>
<td>Gunjal</td>
<td>aaditi@gmail.com</td>
</tr>
<tr>
<td>Spandan</td>
<td>Gite</td>
<td>spandan@gmail.com</td>
</tr>
<tr>
<td>Kavya</td>
<td>Kanjode</td>
<td>kavya@gmail.com</td>
</tr>
</tbody>
</table>
</div>
</div>
</div>
</body>
</html>
```

Tables

Bordered Table

Firstname	Lastname	Email
Taniya	Sevakramani	taniya@gmail.com
Aaditi	Gunjal	aaditi@gmail.com
Spandan	Gite	spandan@gmail.com
Kavya	Kanjode	kavya@gmail.com

Program Output 9.1- Bordered Table.

9.3- Write a program to display Borderless Table.

```
<html>
<head>
<title>Bootstrap - Tables</title>
<link      href="https://cdn.jsdelivr.net/npm/bootstrap@5.1.3/dist/css/bootstrap.min.css" rel="stylesheet">
<script     src="https://cdn.jsdelivr.net/npm/bootstrap@5.1.3/dist/js/bootstrap.bundle.min.js"></script>
</head>
<body>
<div class="container">
<h1>Tables</h1>
<p>Borderless Table</p>
<div class="row">
<div class="col-sm-6">
<table class="table table-borderless">
<thead>
<tr>
<th>Firstname</th>
<th>Lastname</th>
<th>Email</th>
</tr>
</thead>
<tbody>
<tr>
```

```html
<td>Taniya</td>
<td>Sevakramani</td>
<td>taniya@gmail.com</td>
</tr>
<tr>
<td>Aaditi</td>
<td>Gunjal</td>
<td>aaditi@gmail.com</td>
</tr>
<tr>
<td>Spandan</td>
<td>Gite</td>
<td>spandan@gmail.com</td>
</tr>
<tr>
<td>Kavya</td>
<td>Kanjode</td>
<td>kavya@gmail.com</td>
</tr>
</tbody>
</table>
</div>
</div>
</div>
</body>
</html>
```

Tables

Borderless Table

Firstname	Lastname	Email
Taniya	Sevakramani	taniya@gmail.com
Aaditi	Gunjal	aaditi@gmail.com
Spandan	Gite	spandan@gmail.com
Kavya	Kanjode	kavya@gmail.com

Program Output 9.3- Borderless Table

9.4- Write a program to display Responsive Table.

```
<html>
<head>
<title>Bootstrap - Tables</title>
<link      href="https://cdn.jsdelivr.net/npm/bootstrap@5.1.3/
dist/css/bootstrap.min.css" rel="stylesheet">
<script     src="https://cdn.jsdelivr.net/npm/bootstrap@5.1.3/
dist/js/bootstrap.bundle.min.js"></script>
</head>
<body>
<div class="container">
<h1>Tables</h1>
<p>Responsive Table</p>
<div class="row">
<div class="col-sm-6">
<table class="table table-responsive">
<thead>
<tr>
<th>Firstname</th>
<th>Lastname</th>
<th>Email</th>
</tr>
</thead>
<tbody>
<tr>
<td>Taniya</td>
<td>Sevakramani</td>
<td>taniya@gmail.com</td>
</tr>
<tr>
<td>Aaditi</td>
<td>Gunjal</td>
<td>aaditi@gmail.com</td>
</tr>
```

```
<tr>
<td>Spandan</td>
<td>Gite</td>
<td>spandan@gmail.com</td>
</tr>
<tr>
<td>Kavya</td>
<td>Kanjode</td>
<td>kavya@gmail.com</td>
</tr>
</tbody>
</table>
</div>
</div>
</div>
</body>
</html>
```

Tables

Responsive Table

Firstname	Lastname	Email
Taniya	Sevakramani	taniya@gmail.com
Aadit	Gunjal	aadit@gmail.com
Spandan	Gite	spandan@gmail.com
Kavya	Kanjode	kavya@gmail.com

Program Output 9.4- Responsive Table.

9.5-Write a program to display Striped Rows Table.

```
<html>
<head>
<title>Bootstrap - Tables</title>
<link   href="https://cdn.jsdelivr.net/npm/bootstrap@5.1.3/
dist/css/bootstrap.min.css" rel="stylesheet">
<script   src="https://cdn.jsdelivr.net/npm/bootstrap@5.1.3/
dist/js/bootstrap.bundle.min.js"></script>
```

```html
</head>
<body>
<div class="container">
<h1>Tables</h1>
<p>Striped Rows Table</p>
<div class="row">
<div class="col-sm-6">
<table class="table table-striped">
<thead>
<tr>
<th>Firstname</th>
<th>Lastname</th>
<th>Email</th>
</tr>
</thead>
<tbody>
<tr>
<td>Taniya</td>
<td>Sevakramani</td>
<td>taniya@gmail.com</td>
</tr>
<tr>
<td>Aaditi</td>
<td>Gunjal</td>
<td>aaditi@gmail.com</td>
</tr>
<tr>
<td>Spandan</td>
<td>Gite</td>
<td>spandan@gmail.com</td>
</tr>
<tr>
<td>Kavya</td>
<td>Kanjode</td>
<td>kavya@gmail.com</td>
```

```
</tr>
</tbody>
</table>
</div>
</div>
</div>
</body>
</html>
```

Tables

Striped Rows Table

Firstname	Lastname	Email
Tanya	Sevakramani	tanya@gmail.com
Aadit	Gunjal	aadit@gmail.com
Spandan	Gite	spandan@gmail.com
Kavya	Kanjode	kavya@gmail.com

Program Output 9.5- Striped Table.

9.6- Write a program to display Hover Rows Table.

```
<html>
<head>
<title>Bootstrap - Tables</title>
<link     href="https://cdn.jsdelivr.net/npm/bootstrap@5.1.3/
dist/css/bootstrap.min.css" rel="stylesheet">
<script     src="https://cdn.jsdelivr.net/npm/bootstrap@5.1.3/
dist/js/bootstrap.bundle.min.js"></script>
</head>
<body>
<div class="container">
<h1>Tables</h1>
<p>Hover Rows Table</p>
<div class="row">
<div class="col-sm-6">
<table class="table table-hover">
<thead>
```

```html
<tr>
<th>Firstname</th>
<th>Lastname</th>
<th>Email</th>
</tr>
</thead>
<tbody>
<tr>
<td>Taniya</td>
<td>Sevakramani</td>
<td>taniya@gmail.com</td>
</tr>
<tr>
<td>Aaditi</td>
<td>Gunjal</td>
<td>aaditi@gmail.com</td>
</tr>
<tr>
<td>Spandan</td>
<td>Gite</td>
<td>spandan@gmail.com</td>
</tr>
<tr>
<td>Kavya</td>
<td>Kanjode</td>
<td>kavya@gmail.com</td>
</tr>
</tbody>
</table>
</div>
</div>
</div>
</body>
</html>
```

Tables

Hover Rows Table

Firstname	Lastname	Email
Taniya	Sevakramani	taniya@gmail.com
Aadit	Gunjal	aadit@gmail.com
Spandan	Gite	spandan@gmail.com
Kavya	Kanjode	kavya@gmail.com

Program Output 9.6- Hover Table.

9.7- Write a program to display Black/Dark Table.

```
<html>
<head>
<title>Bootstrap - Tables</title>
<link href="https://cdn.jsdelivr.net/npm/bootstrap@5.1.3/dist/css/bootstrap.min.css" rel="stylesheet">
<script src="https://cdn.jsdelivr.net/npm/bootstrap@5.1.3/dist/js/bootstrap.bundle.min.js"></script>
</head>
<body>
<div class="container">
<h1>Tables</h1>
<p>Black/Dark Table</p>
<div class="row">
<div class="col-sm-6">
<table class="table table-dark">
<thead>
<tr>
<th>Firstname</th>
<th>Lastname</th>
<th>Email</th>
</tr>
</thead>
<tbody>
<tr>
<td>Taniya</td>
```

```
<td>Sevakramani</td>
<td>taniya@gmail.com</td>
</tr>
<tr>
<td>Aaditi</td>
<td>Gunjal</td>
<td>aaditi@gmail.com</td>
</tr>
<tr>
<td>Spandan</td>
<td>Gite</td>
<td>spandan@gmail.com</td>
</tr>
<tr>
<td>Kavya</td>
<td>Kanjode</td>
<td>kavya@gmail.com</td>
</tr>
</tbody>
</table>
</div>
</div>
</div>
</body>
</html>
```

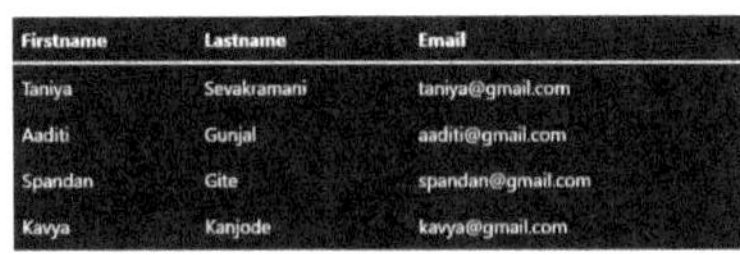

Program Output 9.7- Black/Dark Table.

9.8- Write a program to display Contextual Classes.

```html
<html>
<head>
<title>Bootstrap - Tables</title>
<link href="https://cdn.jsdelivr.net/npm/bootstrap@5.1.3/dist/css/bootstrap.min.css" rel="stylesheet">
<script src="https://cdn.jsdelivr.net/npm/bootstrap@5.1.3/dist/js/bootstrap.bundle.min.js"></script>
</head>
<body>
<div class="container">
<h1>Tables</h1>
<p>Contextual classes Table</p>
<div class="row">
<div class="col-sm-6">
<table class="table">
<thead>
<tr>
<th>Firstname</th>
<th>Lastname</th>
<th>Email</th>
</tr>
</thead>
<tbody>
<tr>
<td>Taniya</td>
<td>Sevakramani</td>
<td>taniya@gmail.com</td>
</tr>
<tr class="table-primary">
<td>Aaditi</td>
<td>Gunjal</td>
<td>aaditi@gmail.com</td>
</tr>
<tr class="table-success">
```

```html
<td>Spandan</td>
<td>Gite</td>
<td>spandan@gmail.com</td>
</tr>
<tr class="table-danger">
<td>Madhuri</td>
<td>Patil</td>
<td>madhuri@gmail.com</td>
</tr>
<tr class="table-info">
<td>Sapna</td>
<td>Gawali</td>
<td>sapana@gmail.com</td>
</tr>
<tr class="table-warning">
<td>Pratiksha</td>
<td>Sharma</td>
<td>pratiksha@gmail.com</td>
</tr>
<tr class="table-active">
<td>Kavya</td>
<td>Kanjode</td>
<td>kavya@gmail.com</td>
</tr>
<tr class="table-secondary">
<td>Samiksha</td>
<td>Dixit</td>
<td>samiksha@gmail.com</td>
</tr>
<tr class="table-light">
<td>Praniti</td>
<td>Bapat</td>
<td>praniti@gmail.com</td>
</tr>
</tbody>
```

```
</table>
</div>
</div>
</div>
</body>
</html>
```

Tables

Contextual classes Table

Firstname	Lastname	Email
Taniya	Sevakramani	taniya@gmail.com
Aaditi	Gunjal	aaditi@gmail.com
Spandan	Gite	spandan@gmail.com
Madhuri	Patil	madhuri@gmail.com
Sapna	Gawali	sapana@gmail.com
Pratiksha	Sharma	pratiksha@gmail.com
Kavya	Kanjode	kavya@gmail.com
Samiksha	Dixit	samiksha@gmail.com
Pranit	Bapat	pranit@gmail.com

Program Output 9.8 Contextual Class Table.

CHAPTER TEN

Buttons

Bootstrap 5 provides various styles of buttons.

10.1 - Write a Program To Show Buttons With Different Class.

```
<html>
<head>
<title>Bootstrap - Buttons</title>
<link href="https://cdn.jsdelivr.net/npm/bootstrap@5.1.3/dist/css/bootstrap.min.css" rel="stylesheet">
<script src="https://cdn.jsdelivr.net/npm/bootstrap@5.1.3/dist/js/bootstrap.bundle.min.js"></script>
</head>
<body>
<div class="container">
<h1>Buttons</h1>
<p>Bootstraps 5 Buttons</p>
<div class="row">
<div class="col-sm-12">
<button type="button" class="btn">Basic</button>
<button type="button" class="btn btn-primary">Primary</button>
<button type="button" class="btn btn-secondary">Secondary</button>
<button type="button" class="btn btn-info">Info</button>
<button type="button" class="btn btn-success">Success</button>
```

```html
<button type="button" class="btn btn-warning">Warning</button>
<button type="button" class="btn btn-danger">Danger</button>
<button type="button" class="btn btn-light">Light</button>
<button type="button" class="btn btn-dark">Dark</button>
<button type="button" class="btn btn-link">Link</button>
</div>
</div>
</div>
</body>
</html>
```

Buttons

Bootstraps 5 Buttons

Basic Primary Secondary Info Success Warning Danger Light Dark Link

Program Output 10.1 - Buttons

10.2 -Write a Bootstrap Program to Show Button Sizes.

```html
<html>
<head>
<title>Bootstrap - Buttons</title>
<link href="https://cdn.jsdelivr.net/npm/bootstrap@5.1.3/dist/css/bootstrap.min.css" rel="stylesheet">
<script src="https://cdn.jsdelivr.net/npm/bootstrap@5.1.3/dist/js/bootstrap.bundle.min.js"></script>
</head>
<body>
<div class="container">
<h1>Buttons</h1>
<p>Bootstraps 5 Button Sizes</p>
<div class="row">
<div class="col-sm-12">
```

```
<button    type="button"    class="btn    btn-info    btn-lg">Large
Button</button>
<button    type="button"    class="btn    btn-primary">Default Size
Button</button>
<button type="button" class="btn btn-secondary btn-sm">Small
Button</button>
</div>
</div>
</div>
</body>
</html>
```

Buttons

Bootstraps 5 Button Sizes

Large Button   Default Size Button   Small Button

Program Output 10.2 - Bootstrap Button Sizes

10.3 - Write a Program to Show Button Outline Styles.

```
<html>
<head>
<title>Bootstrap - Buttons</title>
<link      href="https://cdn.jsdelivr.net/npm/bootstrap@5.1.3/
dist/css/bootstrap.min.css" rel="stylesheet">
<script     src="https://cdn.jsdelivr.net/npm/bootstrap@5.1.3/
dist/js/bootstrap.bundle.min.js"></script>
</head>
<body>
<div class="container">
<h1>Buttons</h1>
<p>Bootstraps 5 Outline Buttons</p>
<div class="row">
<div class="col-sm-12">
<button       type="button"       class="btn       btn-outline-
primary">Primary</button>
```

```
<button type="button" class="btn btn-outline-secondary">Secondary</button>
<button type="button" class="btn btn-outline-info">Info</button>
<button type="button" class="btn btn-outline-success">Success</button>
<button type="button" class="btn btn-outline-warning">Warning</button>
<button type="button" class="btn btn-outline-danger">Danger</button>
<button type="button" class="btn btn-outline-light">Light</button>
<button type="button" class="btn btn-outline-dark">Dark</button>
</div>
</div>
</div>
</body>
</html>
```

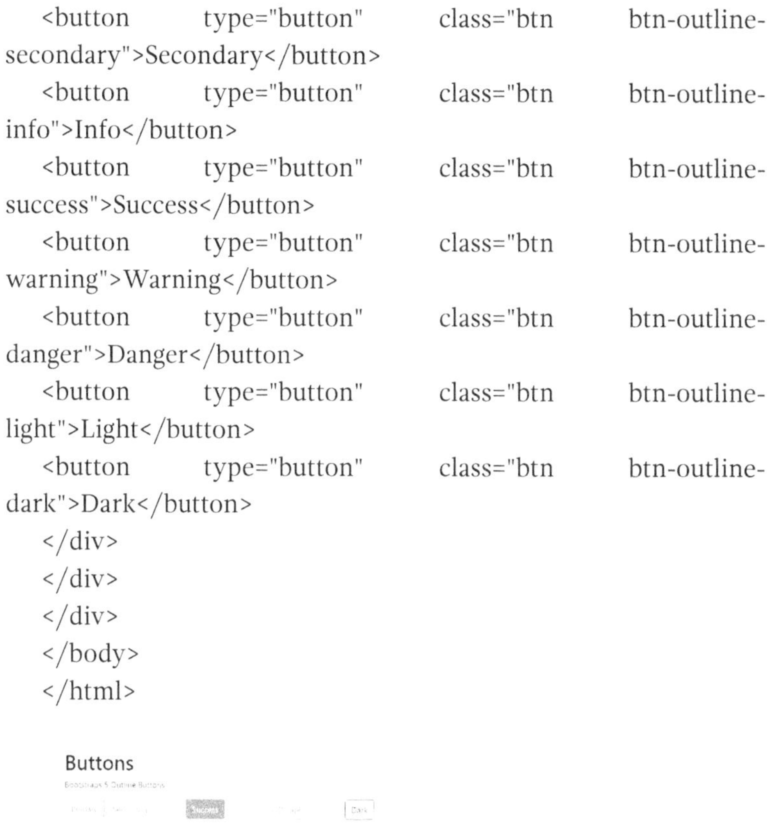

Program Output 10.3 - Outline Buttons

Active, Disabled and Block level buttons

Buttons having active state using active class and disabled using disabled attributes. By .active class button can be shown as button appears pressed and disabled shows button unclick able. **Block level buttons** means full width of parent element of button. By using d-grid class apply on parent element and btn-block class on button. We can create Block level button.

```
<html>
<head>
```

```html
<title>Bootstrap - Buttons</title>
<link href="https://cdn.jsdelivr.net/npm/bootstrap@5.1.3/dist/css/bootstrap.min.css" rel="stylesheet">
<script src="https://cdn.jsdelivr.net/npm/bootstrap@5.1.3/dist/js/bootstrap.bundle.min.js"></script>
</head>
<body>
<div class="container">
<h1>Buttons</h1>
<div class="row">
<div class="col-sm-12">
<button type="button" class="btn btn-primary active">Primary Active</button>
<button type="button" class="btn btn-secondary" disabled>Disabled Button</button>
</div>
</div>
</br>
<div class="col-sm-12">
<div class="d-grid">
<button type="button" class="btn btn-info btn-block">Full-Width Button</button>
</div>
</div>
</div>
</body>
</html>
```

Buttons

Bootstraps 5 Outline Buttons

Primary Active Disabled Button

Full-Width Button

10.4 Program Output - Button Status

CHAPTER ELEVEN

Button Groups

Button Groups - Button groups are a group of buttons in a line. Button groups design in two ways –

1. **Horizontal Button Groups**
2. **Vertical Button Groups**

Horizontal Button Group

11.1 - Write a Bootstrap Program to Show Horizontal Button Groups.

```
<html>
<head>
<title>Bootstrap - Button Groups</title>
<link href="https://cdn.jsdelivr.net/npm/bootstrap@5.1.3/dist/css/bootstrap.min.css" rel="stylesheet">
<script src="https://cdn.jsdelivr.net/npm/bootstrap@5.1.3/dist/js/bootstrap.bundle.min.js"></script>
</head>
<body>
<div class="container">
<h1>Button Groups</h1>
<p>Bootstraps 5 Horizontal Button Groups</p>
<div class="row">
<div class="col-sm-6">
<div class="btn-group">
```

```
<button           type="button"           class="btn           btn-
success">Drawing</button>
<button           type="button"           class="btn           btn-
success">Games</button>
<button   type="button"   class="btn   btn-success">Arts   and
Crafts</button>
<button     type="button"     class="btn     btn-success">Study
Material</button>
</div>
</div>
</div>
</div>
</body>
</html>
```

Button Groups

Bootstraps 5 Horizontal Button Groups

Drawing   Games   Arts and Crafts   Study Material

Program Output 11.1 - Horizontal Button Groups.

Vertical Button Group
Write a Bootstrap Program to Show Vertical Button Groups.

```
<html>
<head>
<title>Bootstrap - Button Groups</title>
<link     href="https://cdn.jsdelivr.net/npm/bootstrap@5.1.3/
dist/css/bootstrap.min.css" rel="stylesheet">
<script    src="https://cdn.jsdelivr.net/npm/bootstrap@5.1.3/
dist/js/bootstrap.bundle.min.js"></script>
</head>
<body>
<div class="container">
<h1>Button Groups</h1>
<p>Bootstraps 5 Vertical Button Groups</p>
```

```
<div class="row">
<div class="col-sm-6">
<div class="btn-group-vertical">
<button type="button" class="btn btn-success">Drawing</button>
<button type="button" class="btn btn-success">Games</button>
<button type="button" class="btn btn-success">Arts and Crafts</button>
<button type="button" class="btn btn-success">Study Material</button>
</div>
</div>
</div>
</div>
</body>
</html>
```

Button Groups

Bootstrap 5 Vertical Button Groups

Drawing
Games
Arts and Crafts
Study Material

Program Output 11.2 Vertical Button Groups.

CHAPTER TWELVE

Labels

Topic Covered

What are Labels

Label component is one of the important components in the bootstrap 5. Bootstrap 5 provides form-label class to display label on the form.

```
<html>
<head>
<title>Bootstrap - Labels</title>
<link href="https://cdn.jsdelivr.net/npm/bootstrap@5.1.3/dist/css/bootstrap.min.css" rel="stylesheet">
<script src="https://cdn.jsdelivr.net/npm/bootstrap@5.1.3/dist/js/bootstrap.bundle.min.js"></script>
</head>
<body>
<div class="container">
<h1>Label</h1>
<p>Introduction to Label</p>
<div class="row">
<div class="col-sm-4">
<label for="name" class="form-label">First Name :</label>
<input type="text" class="form-control" id="fname" placeholder="Enter First Name" name="fname">
</div>
<div class="col-sm-4">
<label for="name" class="form-label">Middle Name:</label>
```

```
    <input       type="text"       class="form-control"       id="mname"
placeholder="Enter Middle Name" name="mname">
    </div>
    <div class="col-sm-4">
    <label for="name" class="form-label">Last Name:</label>
    <input       type="text"       class="form-control"       id="lname"
placeholder="Enter Last Name" name="lname">
    </div>
    </div>
    </div>
    </body>
    </html>
```

Label component used to display more information about the field.

Program Output 12.1 - Display Labels.

CHAPTER THIRTEEN

Dropdowns

Topics Covered –

What are Dropdowns

In Bootstrap 5, dropdown component is displayed to select or choose one option from the suggested list using dropdown class with div. Let us learn some of the dropdown classes.

dropdown class – To create the dropdown component.

dropdown-toggle class – To open dropdown menu using button or link with dropdown-toggle class.

dropdown-menu class – It is used to create the dropdown menu list.

dropdown-item class – To add item in the dropdown menu dropdown-item class is used.

13.1 - Write a Bootstrap Program to Show Dropdown list of Subjects.

```
<html>
<head>
<title>Bootstrap - Dropdowns</title>
<link href="https://cdn.jsdelivr.net/npm/bootstrap@5.1.3/dist/css/bootstrap.min.css" rel="stylesheet">
<script src="https://cdn.jsdelivr.net/npm/bootstrap@5.1.3/dist/js/bootstrap.bundle.min.js"></script>
</head>
<body>
<div class="container">
<h1>Dropdown</h1>
```

```
<p>Introduction to Dropdowns</p>
<div class="row">
<div class="col-sm-4">
<div class="dropdown">
<button type="button" class="btn btn-secondary dropdown-toggle" data-bs-toggle="dropdown">
Subject List
</button>
<ul class="dropdown-menu">
<li><a class="dropdown-item" href="#">Marathi</a></li>
<li><a class="dropdown-item" href="#">Hindi</a></li>
<li><a class="dropdown-item" href="#">English</a></li>
<li><a class="dropdown-item" href="#">Science</a></li>
<li><a class="dropdown-item" href="#">Maths</a></li>
<li><a class="dropdown-item" href="#">Computer</a></li>
<li><a class="dropdown-item" href="#">History</a></li>
</ul>
</div>
</div>
</div>
</div>
</body>
</html>
```

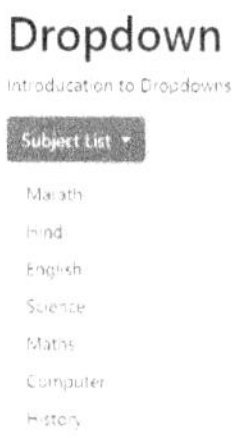

Program Output 13.1 - Display Subject List in Dropdown.

CHAPTER FOURTEEN

Glyphicons

Glyphicons are the Icons in the form of fonts used in the web and app design purpose.

Following are some examples of the Glyphicons –

14.1 - Write a Program introduction to Bootstrap - Glyphicons

```
<html>
<head>
<title>Bootstrap - Glyphicons</title>
<link rel="stylesheet" href="https://maxcdn.bootstrapcdn.com/bootstrap/3.3.6/css/bootstrap.min.css">
<script src="https://ajax.googleapis.com/ajax/libs/jquery/1.12.0/jquery.min.js"></script>
<script src="https://maxcdn.bootstrapcdn.com/bootstrap/3.3.6/js/bootstrap.min.js"></script>
</head>
<body>
<div class="container">
<h1>Glyphicons</h1>
<p>Diffrent Glyphicons</p>
<div class="row">
<div class="col-lg-3">
<p>Envelope icon: <span class="glyphicon glyphicon-ok"></span></p>
</div>
<div class="col-lg-3">
<p>Music icon: <span class="glyphicon glyphicon-
```

```html
music"></span></p>
</div>
<div class="col-lg-3">
<p>Time icon: <span class="glyphicon glyphicon-time"></span></p>
</div>
<div class="col-lg-3">
<p>Pencil icon: <span class="glyphicon glyphicon-pencil"></span></p>
</div>
</div>
<div class="row">
<div class="col-sm-3">
<p>QR Code icon: <span class="glyphicon glyphicon-qrcode"></span></p>
</div>
<div class="col-sm-3">
<p>Camera icon: <span class="glyphicon glyphicon-camera"></span></p>
</div>
<div class="col-sm-3">
<p>Globe icon: <span class="glyphicon glyphicon-globe"></span></p>
</div>
<div class="col-sm-3">
<p>Send icon: <span class="glyphicon glyphicon-send"></span></p>
</div>
</div>
</div>
</body>
</html>
```

Glyphicons

Diffrent Glyphicons

Ok icon ✔   Music icon ♪   Time icon ⊙   Pencil icon ✎

QR Code icon ▤   Camera icon 📷   Globe icon 🌐   Send icon ◀

Program Output 14.1 - Glyphicons

CHAPTER FIFTEEN

List Groups

Topics covered –

What is List

List are displayed in the form of groups in List Group Components. Basic List Group form in using following classes.

list-group – To design Basic List Group list-group class is used with <ul> or <ol> elements.

list-group-item - To add items in list list-group-item class is used with <li> element.

The basic List Group is formed using unordered list.

15.1 - Write a Bootstrap Program to Show List Group.

```
<html>
<head>
<title>Bootstrap - List Groups</title>
<link href="https://cdn.jsdelivr.net/npm/bootstrap@5.1.3/dist/css/bootstrap.min.css" rel="stylesheet">
<script src="https://cdn.jsdelivr.net/npm/bootstrap@5.1.3/dist/js/bootstrap.bundle.min.js"></script>
</head>
<body>
<div class="container">
<h1>List Groups</h1>
<p>Bootstraps 5 List Groups</p>
<div class="row">
<div class="col-sm-6">
<ul class="list-group">
```

```
<li class="list-group-item">Golden Group</li>
<li class="list-group-item">Silver Group</li>
<li class="list-group-item">Bronze Group</li>
<li class="list-group-item">Platinum Group</li>
</ul>
</div>
</div>
</div>
</body>
</html>
```

List Groups

Bootstraps 5 List Groups

Golden Group

Silver Group

Bronze Group

Platinum Group

Program Output 15.1 - List Groups

CHAPTER SIXTEEN

Jumbotron

Topics covered –

What is Jumbotron

Jumbotron is a big box or text banner with color background. Unfortunately, it is no longer in bootstrap 5. It was launched in bootstrap 3. The purpose of jumbotron is to display or create important information or content. We can create same banner using some classes with div element.

16.1 - Write a Bootstrap Program to Show Jumbotron

```
<html>
<head>
<title>Bootstrap - Jumbotron</title>
<link href="https://cdn.jsdelivr.net/npm/bootstrap@5.1.3/dist/css/bootstrap.min.css" rel="stylesheet">
<script src="https://cdn.jsdelivr.net/npm/bootstrap@5.1.3/dist/js/bootstrap.bundle.min.js"></script>
</head>
<body>
<div class="container">
<h1>Jumbotron</h1>
<p>Bootstraps 5 Jumbotron</p>
<div class="p-5 bg-secondary text-white rounded">
<h1>Happy Life</h1>
<p>Happy life.Happy life.Happy life.Happy life.Happy life.Happy life.Happy life.Happy life.Happy life.Happy life.Happy life.Happy life.Happy life.Happy life.Happy life.Happy
```

life.Happy life.Happy life.Happy life.Happy life.Happy life.Happy life.Happy life.Happy life.</p>

```
    </div>
    </div>
    </body>
    </html>
```

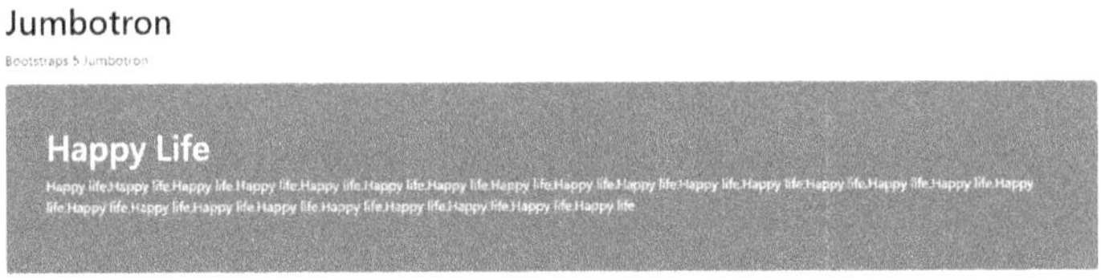

Program Output 16.1 - Jumbotron Example

CHAPTER SEVENTEEN

Badges

Topics covered –

What are badges?

In bootstrap **Badges** are used to provide or display extra information in content. To display such information badge class is used with other classes.

To create rectangular badges span elements are used.

17.1 - Write a Bootstrap Program to Show a Rectangular Badges.

```
<html>
<head>
<title>Bootstrap - Badges</title>
<link     href="https://cdn.jsdelivr.net/npm/bootstrap@5.1.3/dist/css/bootstrap.min.css" rel="stylesheet">
<script     src="https://cdn.jsdelivr.net/npm/bootstrap@5.1.3/dist/js/bootstrap.bundle.min.js"></script>
</head>
<body>
<div class="container">
<h1>Badges</h1>
<p>Bootstraps 5 Badges</p>
<div class="row">
<div class="col-sm-6">
<h4>Subject and Marks obtained in subjects</h5>
<h6>Marathi <span class="badge bg-primary">89</span></h6>
<h6>English <span class="badge bg-primary">80</span></h6>
```

```
<h6>History <span class="badge bg-primary">92</span></h6>
<h6>Computer <span class="badge bg-primary">95</span></h6>
<h6>Science <span class="badge bg-primary">97</span></h6>
<h6>Hindi <span class="badge bg-primary">86</span></h6>
</div>
</div>
</div>
</body>
</html>
```

Program Output 17.1 - Badges Example

Rounded Pill Badges
Write a Bootstrap Program to Show Rounded Pill Badges.

```
<html>
<head>
<title>Bootstrap - Badges</title>
<link href="https://cdn.jsdelivr.net/npm/bootstrap@5.1.3/dist/css/bootstrap.min.css" rel="stylesheet">
<script src="https://cdn.jsdelivr.net/npm/bootstrap@5.1.3/dist/js/bootstrap.bundle.min.js"></script>
</head>
<body>
<div class="container">
<h1>Badges</h1>
<p>Bootstraps 5 Rounded Pill Badges</p>
<div class="row">
```

```
<div class="col-sm-6">
<h6>----- <span class="badge rounded-pill bg-success">Marathi</span></h6>
<h6>----- <span class="badge rounded-pill bg-success">English</span></h6>
<h6>----- <span class="badge rounded-pill bg-success">Hindi</span></h6>
<h6>----- <span class="badge rounded-pill bg-success">History</span></h6>
<h6>----- <span class="badge rounded-pill bg-success">Computer</span></h6>
<h6>----- <span class="badge rounded-pill bg-success">Science</span></h6>
<h6>----- <span class="badge rounded-pill bg-success">Art and Crafts</span></h6>
<h6>----- <span class="badge rounded-pill bg-success">Drawing</span></h6>
</div>
</div>
</div>
</body>
</html>
```


Program Output 17.2 - Rounded Pill Badges

17.3 -Write a Bootstrap Program to show Contextual Badges

```
<html>
<head>
```

```html
<title>Bootstrap - Badges</title>
<link       href="https://cdn.jsdelivr.net/npm/bootstrap@5.1.3/
dist/css/bootstrap.min.css" rel="stylesheet">
<script      src="https://cdn.jsdelivr.net/npm/bootstrap@5.1.3/
dist/js/bootstrap.bundle.min.js"></script>
</head>
<body>
<div class="container">
<h1>Badges</h1>
<p>Bootstraps 5 Contextual Badges</p>
<div class="row">
<div class="col-sm-6">
<h6>-      <span      class="badge      rounded-pill      bg-
Primary">Marathi</span></h6>
<h6>-      <span      class="badge      rounded-pill      bg-
secondary">English</span></h6>
<h6>-      <span      class="badge      rounded-pill      bg-
info">Hindi</span></h6>
<h6>-      <span      class="badge      rounded-pill      bg-
success">History</span></h6>
<h6>-      <span      class="badge      rounded-pill      bg-
warning">Computer</span></h6>
<h6>-      <span      class="badge      rounded-pill      bg-
danger">Science</span></h6>
<h6>- <span class="badge rounded-pill bg-dark">Art   and
Crafts</span></h6>
</div>
</div>
</div>
</body>
</html>
```

Program Output 17.3 - Contextual Badges

CHAPTER EIGHTEEN

Alerts

In bootstrap Alerts are created using alert class. We can produce different alerts with the help of contextual classes also.

18.1 - Write a Bootstrap Program to Show Alerts with Different Classes.

```
<html>
<head>
<title>Bootstrap - Alerts</title>
<link href="https://cdn.jsdelivr.net/npm/bootstrap@5.1.3/dist/css/bootstrap.min.css" rel="stylesheet">
<script src="https://cdn.jsdelivr.net/npm/bootstrap@5.1.3/dist/js/bootstrap.bundle.min.js"></script>
</head>
<body>
<div class="container">
<h1>Alerts</h1>
<p>Bootstraps 5 Alerts</p>
<div class="row">
<div class="col-sm-6">
<div class="alert alert-primary">
<strong>Alert Message!</strong> with class primary.
</div>
<div class="alert alert-secondary">
<strong>Alert Message!</strong> with class secondary.
</div>
<div class="alert alert-info">
```

```
<strong>Alert Message!</strong> with class info.
</div>
<div class="alert alert-success">
<strong>Alert Message!</strong> with class success.
</div>
<div class="alert alert-danger">
<strong>Alert Message!</strong> with class danger.
</div>
<div class="alert alert-warning">
<strong>Alert Message!</strong> with class warning.
</div>
</div>
</div>
</div>
</body>
</html>
```

Alerts

Bootstrap 5 Alerts

Alert Message! with class primary.

Alert Message! with class secondary.

Alert Message! with class info.

Alert Message! with class success.

Alert Message! with class danger.

Alert Message! with class warning.

Program Output 18.1 - Alerts Example

18.2 - Write a Bootstrap Program to Show Alerts with Close Button.

```
<html>
<head>
<title>Bootstrap - Alerts</title>
```

```html
<link href="https://cdn.jsdelivr.net/npm/bootstrap@5.1.3/dist/css/bootstrap.min.css" rel="stylesheet">
<script src="https://cdn.jsdelivr.net/npm/bootstrap@5.1.3/dist/js/bootstrap.bundle.min.js"></script>
</head>
<body>
<div class="container">
<h1>Closing Alerts</h1>
<p>Bootstraps 5 Closing Alerts</p>
<div class="row">
<div class="col-sm-6">
<div class="alert alert-info alert-dismissible">
<button type="button" class="btn-close" data-bs-dismiss="alert"></button>
<strong>Save!</strong> Record saved successfully.
</div>
<div class="alert alert-success alert-dismissible">
<button type="button" class="btn-close" data-bs-dismiss="alert"></button>
<strong>Success!</strong> User registered successfully.
</div>
</div>
</div>
</div>
</body>
</html>
```

Closing Alerts

Bootstraps 5 Closing Alerts

Save! Record saved successfully.   ✕

Success! User registered successfully.   ✕

Program Output 18.2 - Closing Alerts

CHAPTER NINETEEN

Panels

Topics covered –

What are Panels

Panel in bootstrap created using panel class with div class.

Panel displayed with contextual classes with panel class. – **panel panel-default.**

Panel heading helps to add heading container in panel.– **panel-heading.**

Panel title is enclosed within panel heading using class – **panel-title.**

Panel content arranged in panel body section using class – **panel-body.**

Panel footer display footer information in footer section using class – **panel-footer.**

19.1 - Write a Bootstrap Program to Display Panels.

```
<html>
<head>
<title>Bootstrap - Panels</title>
<link href="https://cdn.jsdelivr.net/npm/bootstrap@5.1.3/dist/css/bootstrap.min.css" rel="stylesheet">
<script src="https://cdn.jsdelivr.net/npm/bootstrap@5.1.3/dist/js/bootstrap.bundle.min.js"></script>
</head>
<body>
<div class="container">
<h1>Panels</h1>
```

```html
<p>Bootstraps 5 Panels</p>
<div class="row">
<div class="col-sm-4">
<div class = "panel panel-primary">
<div class = "panel-heading">
<h5 class = "panel-title">
Panel Title
</h5>
</div>
<div class = "panel-body">
Bootstrap panel body used to display the content of the panel.
</div>
<div class = "panel-footer">
Panel Footer Section
</div>
</div>
</div>
</div>
</div>
</body>
</html>
```

Panels

Bootstraps 5 Panels

Panel Title

Bootstrap panel body used to display the content of the
panel.
Panel Footer Section

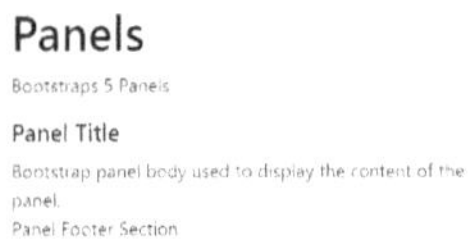

Program Output 19.1 - Panels

CHAPTER TWENTY

Cards

In bootstrap 5 to display content in bordered box card class used. It appears on the screen as a bordered box with content and different colors combination. Card having different section like header, body and footer.

20.1 - Write a Bootstrap Program to Display Cards.

```html
<html>
<head>
<title>Bootstrap - Cards</title>
<link    href="https://cdn.jsdelivr.net/npm/bootstrap@5.1.3/dist/css/bootstrap.min.css" rel="stylesheet">
<script   src="https://cdn.jsdelivr.net/npm/bootstrap@5.1.3/dist/js/bootstrap.bundle.min.js"></script>
</head>
<body>
<div class="container">
<h1>Cards</h1>
<p>Bootstraps 5 Cards</p>

<div class="row">
<div class="col-sm-4">
    <div class = "card">
<div class = "card-header">
Card Header
</div>
```

```
<div class = "card-body">
Bootstrap card body section used to display the content of the card.
</div>
   <div class = "card-footer">
Card Footer Section
</div>
</div>
   </div>
</div>
   </div>
</body>
</html>
```

Cards

Bootstraps 5 Cards

Card Header

Bootstrap card body section used to display the content of the card

Card Footer Section

Program Output 20.1 - Cards

20.2 - Write a Program to Display Cards with Contextual Classes.

```
<html>
<head>
<title>Bootstrap - Cards</title>
<link    href="https://cdn.jsdelivr.net/npm/bootstrap@5.1.3/
dist/css/bootstrap.min.css" rel="stylesheet">
<script    src="https://cdn.jsdelivr.net/npm/bootstrap@5.1.3/
dist/js/bootstrap.bundle.min.js"></script>
</head>
<body>
<div class="container">
<h1>Cards</h1>
```

<p>Bootstraps 5 Cards</p>
<div class="row">
<div class="col-sm-4">
<div class = "card bg-primary text-white">
<div class = "card-header">
Card Header
</div>
<div class = "card-body">
Bootstrap card body section used to display the content of the card.
</div>
<div class = "card-footer">
Card Footer Section
</div>
</div>
</div>
<div class="col-sm-4">
<div class = "card bg-secondary text-white">
<div class = "card-header">
Card Header
</div>
<div class = "card-body">
Bootstrap card body section used to display the content of the card.
</div>
<div class = "card-footer">
Card Footer Section
</div>
</div>
</div>
<div class="col-sm-4">
<div class = "card bg-info text-white">
<div class = "card-header">
Card Header
</div>

<div class = "card-body">
Bootstrap card body section used to display the content of the card.
</div>
<div class = "card-footer">
Card Footer Section
</div>
</div>
</div>
</div>
</br>
<div class="row">
<div class="col-sm-4">
<div class = "card bg-success text-white">
<div class = "card-header">
Card Header
</div>
<div class = "card-body">
Bootstrap card body section used to display the content of the card.
</div>
<div class = "card-footer">
Card Footer Section
</div>
</div>
</div>
<div class="col-sm-4">
<div class = "card bg-danger text-white">
<div class = "card-header">
Card Header
</div>
<div class = "card-body">
Bootstrap card body section used to display the content of the card.
</div>

```
<div class = "card-footer">
Card Footer Section
</div>
</div>
</div>
<div class="col-sm-4">
<div class = "card bg-warning text-white">
<div class = "card-header">
Card Header
</div>
<div class = "card-body">
Bootstrap card body section used to display the content of the
card.
</div>
<div class = "card-footer">
Card Footer Section
</div>
</div>
</div>
</div>
</div>
</div>
</body>
</html>
```

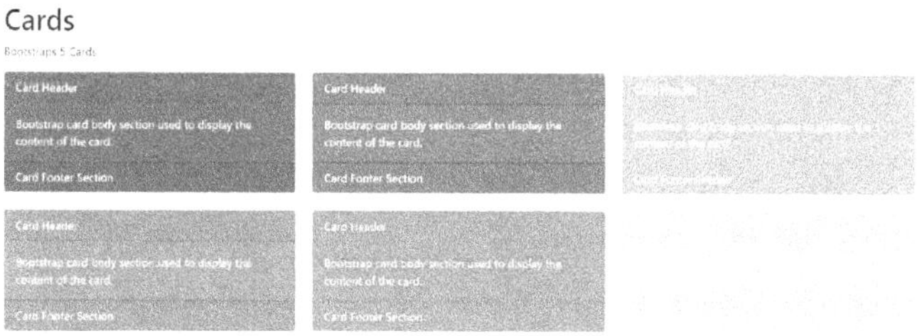

Program Output 20.2 - Cards with contextual classes.

CHAPTER TWENTY-ONE

Breadcrumbs

Breadcrumbs are specially used for navigation purpose by using **breadcrumb** class. To add navigation elements in the list **breadcrumb-item** class is used.

21.1 - Write a Bootstrap Program to Show Breadcrumbs.

```
<html>
<head>
<title>Bootstrap - Breadcrumbs</title>
<link href="https://cdn.jsdelivr.net/npm/bootstrap@5.1.3/dist/css/bootstrap.min.css" rel="stylesheet">
<script src="https://cdn.jsdelivr.net/npm/bootstrap@5.1.3/dist/js/bootstrap.bundle.min.js"></script>
</head>
<body>
<div class="container">
<h1>Breadcrumbs</h1>
<p>Bootstraps 5 Breadcrumbs</p>
<div class="row">
<div class="col-sm-4">
<nav aria-label="breadcrumb">
<ol class="breadcrumb">
<li class="breadcrumb-item"><a href="#">Home</a></li>
<li class="breadcrumb-item"><a href="#">Board</a></li>
<li class="breadcrumb-item"><a href="#">Class</a></li>
<li class="breadcrumb-item"><a href="#">Subject</a></li>
```

```
<li            class="breadcrumb-item            active"            aria-
current="page">Topics</li>
</ol>
</nav>
</div>
</div>
</div>
</body>
</html>
```

Breadcrumbs

Bootstraps 5 Breadcrumbs

Home   Board   Class   subject   Topic

Program Output 21.1 - Breadcrumbs Example

CHAPTER TWENTY-TWO

Tooltips

To provide additional information to user in pop-up box format, tooltips used. When user hover mouse pointer on element like button tooltip will appears. It provides information using tooltip class in bootstrap 5.

22.1 - Write a Bootstrap Program to Show Tooltips.

```
<html>
<head>
<title>Bootstrap - Tooltips</title>
<link href="https://cdn.jsdelivr.net/npm/bootstrap@5.1.3/dist/css/bootstrap.min.css" rel="stylesheet">
<script src="https://cdn.jsdelivr.net/npm/bootstrap@5.1.3/dist/js/bootstrap.bundle.min.js"></script>
</head>
<body>
<div class="container">
<h1>Tooltips</h1>
<p>Bootstraps 5 Tooltips</p>
<div class="row">
<div class="col-sm-4">
<button type="button" class="btn btn-success" data-bs-toggle="tooltip" title="Click on button for registration.">Register</button>
</div>
</div>
</div>
```

```
<script>
var                    tooltipTriggerList                    =
[].slice.call(document.querySelectorAll('[data-bs-
toggle="tooltip"]'))
var     tooltipList     =     tooltipTriggerList.map(function
(tooltipTriggerEl) {
return new bootstrap.Tooltip(tooltipTriggerEl)
})
</script>
</body>
</html>
```


Program Output 22.1 - Display Tooltips

Tooltip Position on Element

To place the tooltip as per requirement like top, bottom, left and right side of the element. data-bs-placement attribute is used to set the position of the tooltip on the element.

22.2 - Write a Bootstrap Program to Display Tooltips.

```
<html>
<head>
<title>Bootstrap - Tooltips</title>
<link     href="https://cdn.jsdelivr.net/npm/bootstrap@5.1.3/
dist/css/bootstrap.min.css" rel="stylesheet">
<script     src="https://cdn.jsdelivr.net/npm/bootstrap@5.1.3/
dist/js/bootstrap.bundle.min.js"></script>
</head>
<body>
<div class="container">
<h1>Tooltips</h1>
<p>Bootstraps 5 Tooltips</p>
```

```
<div class="row">
<div class="col-sm-4">
<button type="button" class="btn btn-success" data-bs-toggle="tooltip" data-bs-placement="top" title="Click on button for registration.">Register</button>
<button type="button" class="btn btn-success" data-bs-toggle="tooltip" data-bs-placement="bottom" title="Click on button for registration.">Register</button>
<button type="button" class="btn btn-success" data-bs-toggle="tooltip" data-bs-placement="left" title="Click on button for registration.">Register</button>
<button type="button" class="btn btn-success" data-bs-toggle="tooltip" data-bs-placement="right" title="Click on button for registration.">Register</button>
</div>
</div>
</div>
<script>
var tooltipTriggerList = [].slice.call(document.querySelectorAll('[data-bs-toggle="tooltip"]'))
var tooltipList = tooltipTriggerList.map(function (tooltipTriggerEl) {
return new bootstrap.Tooltip(tooltipTriggerEl)
})
</script>
</body>
</html>
```

Program Output 22.2 - Tooltips position

CHAPTER TWENTY-THREE

Navbar

Navigation Bar is used to navigate the pages of website from home or main page. In bootstrap 5 navbar class is used to design Navigation bar.

23.1 - Write a Bootstrap Program to Display Navigation Bar.

```html
<html>
<head>
<title>Bootstrap - NavigationBar</title>
<link href="https://cdn.jsdelivr.net/npm/bootstrap@5.1.3/dist/css/bootstrap.min.css" rel="stylesheet">
<script src="https://cdn.jsdelivr.net/npm/bootstrap@5.1.3/dist/js/bootstrap.bundle.min.js"></script>
</head>
<body>
<div class="container">
<h1>NavigationBar</h1>
<p>Bootstrap 5 NavigationBar</p>
<nav class="navbar navbar-expand-sm bg-success">
<div class="container-fluid">
<ul class="navbar-nav">
<li class="nav-item">
<a class="nav-link text-white active" href="#">Home</a>
</li>
<li class="nav-item">
<a class="nav-link text-white" href="#">Water</a>
</li>
```

```
<li class="nav-item">
<a class="nav-link text-white" href="#">Photo Gallery</a>
</li>
<li class="nav-item">
<a class="nav-link text-white" href="#">Feedback</a>
</li>
<li class="nav-item">
<a class="nav-link text-white" href="#">Contact Us</a>
</li>
</ul>
</div>
</nav>
</div>
</body>
</html>
```


Program Output 23.1 - Horizontal Navigation Bar

23.2 - Write a Program to show Vertical Navigation Bar.

```
<html>
<head>
<title>Bootstrap - Navigation Bar</title>
<link      href="https://cdn.jsdelivr.net/npm/bootstrap@5.1.3/
dist/css/bootstrap.min.css" rel="stylesheet">
<script     src="https://cdn.jsdelivr.net/npm/bootstrap@5.1.3/
dist/js/bootstrap.bundle.min.js"></script>
</head>
<body>
<div class="container">
<h1>Navigation Bar</h1>
```

```html
<p>Bootstrap 5 Vertical Navigation Bar</p>
<nav class="navbar bg-info">
<div class="container-fluid">
<ul class="navbar-nav">
<li class="nav-item">
<a class="nav-link text-white active" href="#">Home</a>
</li>
<li class="nav-item">
<a class="nav-link text-white" href="#">Water</a>
</li>
<li class="nav-item">
<a class="nav-link text-white" href="#">Photo Gallery</a>
</li>
<li class="nav-item">
<a class="nav-link text-white" href="#">Feedback</a>
</li>
<li class="nav-item">
<a class="nav-link text-white" href="#">Contact Us</a>
</li>
</ul>
</div>
</nav>
</div>
</body>
</html>
```

Program Output 23.2 - Vertical Navigation Bar

CHAPTER TWENTY-FOUR

Carousal

Carousal is also called as slideshow which appear on top of web page. It is used to display information with picture and text format.

24.1 - Write a Bootstrap Program to Display Carousal.

```
<html>
<head>
<title>Bootstrap - Carousal</title>
<link href="https://cdn.jsdelivr.net/npm/bootstrap@5.1.3/dist/css/bootstrap.min.css" rel="stylesheet">
<script src="https://cdn.jsdelivr.net/npm/bootstrap@5.1.3/dist/js/bootstrap.bundle.min.js"></script>
</head>
<body>
<div class="container">
<h1>Carousal</h1>
<p>Bootstraps 5 Carousal</p>
<div id="demo" class="carousel slide" data-bs-ride="carousel">
<!-- Bottom slide image indicator-->
<div class="carousel-indicators">
<button type="button" data-bs-target="#carousel" data-bs-slide-to="0" class="active"></button>
<button type="button" data-bs-target="#carousel" data-bs-slide-to="1"></button>
<button type="button" data-bs-target="#carousel" data-bs-slide-to="2"></button>
</div>
```

```html
<!-- Carousel or Slideshow -->
<div class="carousel-inner">
<div class="carousel-item active">
<img src="banner1.JPG" alt="Los Angeles" class="d-block w-100">
</div>
<div class="carousel-item">
<img src="banner2.JPEG" alt="Chicago" class="d-block w-100">
</div>
<div class="carousel-item">
<img src="banner3.JPG" alt="New York" class="d-block w-100">
</div>
</div>
<!-- Left and right arrows icons -->
<button class="carousel-control-prev" type="button" data-bs-target="#demo" data-bs-slide="prev">
<span class="carousel-control-prev-icon"></span>
</button>
<button class="carousel-control-next" type="button" data-bs-target="#demo" data-bs-slide="next">
<span class="carousel-control-next-icon"></span>
</button>
</div>
</div>
</body>
</html>
```

Carousal

Bootstraps 5 Carousal

Program Output 24.1 - Carousal

CHAPTER TWENTY-FIVE

Modal

Modal box is rectangular pop-up box or window created using **modal** class with div element. it is open using button component or link.

25.1 - Write a Bootstrap Program to Show Modal.

```
<html>
<head>
<title>Bootstrap - Modal</title>
<link href="https://cdn.jsdelivr.net/npm/bootstrap@5.1.3/dist/css/bootstrap.min.css" rel="stylesheet">
<script src="https://cdn.jsdelivr.net/npm/bootstrap@5.1.3/dist/js/bootstrap.bundle.min.js"></script>
</head>
<body>
<div class="container">
<h1>Modal</h1>
<p>Bootstraps 5 Modal</p>
<div class="row">
<div class="col-sm-4">
<button type="button" class="btn btn-info" data-bs-toggle="modal" data-bs-target="#showModal">
Show Modal
</button>
<!-- The Modal -->
<div class="modal" id="showModal">
<div class="modal-dialog">
```

```
<div class="modal-content">
<!-- Modal Header -->
<div class="modal-header">
<h4 class="modal-title">Bootstrap 5 Modal</h4>
<button type="button" class="btn-close" data-bs-dismiss="modal"></button>
</div>
<!-- Modal body -->
<div class="modal-body">
Welcome to Bootstrap Modal Box.
</div>
<!-- Modal footer -->
<div class="modal-footer">
<button type="button" class="btn btn-warning" data-bs-dismiss="modal">Close</button>
</div>
</div>
</div>
</div>
</div>
</div>
</div>
</div>
</body>
</html>
```

Program Output 25.1 - Modal Example

CHAPTER TWENTY-SIX

Progress Bar

Progress Bar is used to show the progress of current activity using progress class with div element and progress-bar class with child element.

26.1 - Write a Bootstrap Program to Show basic Progress bar.

Basic Progress bar

```
<html>
<head>
<title>Bootstrap - Progress Bar</title>
<link href="https://cdn.jsdelivr.net/npm/bootstrap@5.1.3/dist/css/bootstrap.min.css" rel="stylesheet">
<script src="https://cdn.jsdelivr.net/npm/bootstrap@5.1.3/dist/js/bootstrap.bundle.min.js"></script>
</head>
<body>
<div class="container">
<h1>Progress Bar</h1>
<p>Bootstraps 5 Progress Bar</p>
<div class="row">
<div class="col-sm-9">
<div class="progress">
<div class="progress-bar" style="width:40%"></div>
</div>
</br>
<div class="progress">
<div class="progress-bar" style="width:65%">65%</div>
```

```
</div>
</div>
</div>
</div>
</body>
</html>
```


Program Output 26.1 - Progress bar

Animated Progress bar
Write a Bootstrap Program to Display Animated ProgressBar.

```
<html>
<head>
<title>Bootstrap - ProgressBar</title>
<link     href="https://cdn.jsdelivr.net/npm/bootstrap@5.1.3/
dist/css/bootstrap.min.css" rel="stylesheet">
<script     src="https://cdn.jsdelivr.net/npm/bootstrap@5.1.3/
dist/js/bootstrap.bundle.min.js"></script>
</head>
<body>
<div class="container">
<h1>Animated ProgressBar</h1>
<p>Bootstraps 5 Animated ProgressBar</p>
<div class="row">
<div class="col-sm-9">
<div class="progress">
<div  class="progress-bar  progress-bar-striped  progress-bar-
animated" style="width:65%">65%</div>
</div>
</div>
```

```
</div>
</div>
</body>
</html>
```

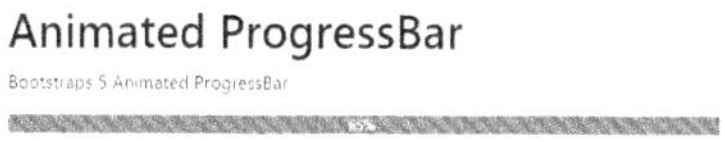

Program Output 26.2 - Animated Progress bar.

Contextual Progress bar

26.3 - Write a Bootstrap Program to Show Progress Bar with Contextual Classes.

```
<html>
<head>
<title>Bootstrap - ProgressBar</title>
<link      href="https://cdn.jsdelivr.net/npm/bootstrap@5.1.3/
dist/css/bootstrap.min.css" rel="stylesheet">
<script    src="https://cdn.jsdelivr.net/npm/bootstrap@5.1.3/
dist/js/bootstrap.bundle.min.js"></script>
</head>
<body>
<div class="container">
<h1>Contextual ProgressBar</h1>
<p>Bootstraps 5 Contextual ProgressBar</p>
<div class="row">
<div class="col-sm-9">
<div class="progress">
<div class="progress-bar" style="width:75%">75%</div>
</div>
</br>
<div class="progress">
<div          class="progress-bar          bg-secondary"
style="width:75%">75%</div>
```

```
    </div>
    </br>
    <div class="progress">
    <div              class="progress-bar              bg-info"
style="width:75%">75%</div>
    </div>
    </br>
    <div class="progress">
    <div              class="progress-bar            bg-success"
style="width:75%">75%</div>
    </div>
    </br>
    <div class="progress">
    <div              class="progress-bar             bg-danger"
style="width:75%">75%</div>
    </div>
    </br>
    <div class="progress">
    <div              class="progress-bar            bg-warning"
style="width:75%">75%</div>
    </div>
    </div>
    </div>
    </div>
    </body>
    </html>
```

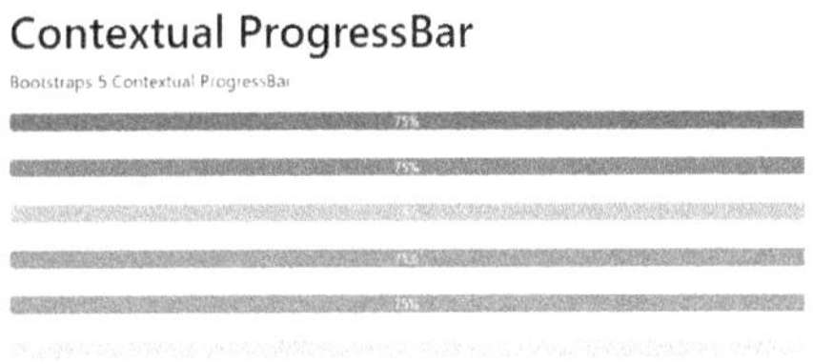

Program Output 26.3 - Progress bar with contextual classes.

Striped Progress Bar

26.4 - Write a Bootstrap Program to Display Striped Progress Bar.

```
<html>
<head>
<title>Bootstrap - ProgressBar</title>
<link       href="https://cdn.jsdelivr.net/npm/bootstrap@5.1.3/
dist/css/bootstrap.min.css" rel="stylesheet">
<script     src="https://cdn.jsdelivr.net/npm/bootstrap@5.1.3/
dist/js/bootstrap.bundle.min.js"></script>
</head>
<body>
<div class="container">
<h1>Striped ProgressBar</h1>
<p>Bootstraps 5 Striped ProgressBar</p>
<div class="row">
<div class="col-sm-9">
<div class="progress">
<div           class="progress-bar          progress-bar-striped"
style="width:75%">75%</div>
</div>
</br>
<div class="progress">
<div  class="progress-bar  progress-bar-striped  bg secondary"
style="width:75%">75%</div>
</div>
</br>
<div class="progress">
<div      class="progress-bar     progress-bar-striped     bg-info"
style="width:75%">75%</div>
</div>
</br>
<div class="progress">
```

```
    <div    class="progress-bar    progress-bar-striped    bg-success"
style="width:75%">75%</div>
    </div>
    </br>
    <div class="progress">
    <div    class="progress-bar    progress-bar-striped    bg-danger"
style="width:75%">75%</div>
    </div>
    </br>
    <div class="progress">
    <div    class="progress-bar    progress-bar-striped    bg-warning"
style="width:75%">75%</div>
    </div>
    </div>
    </div>
    </div>
    </body>
    </html>
```

Program Output 26.4 - Striped Progress bar